THE JPS B'NAI MITZVAH TORAH COMMENTARY

Mikkets (Genesis 41:1–44:17)
Haftarah (1 Kings 3:15–28; 4:1)

Rabbi Jeffrey K. Salkin

The Jewish Publication Society · Philadelphia
University of Nebraska Press · Lincoln

INTRODUCTION

News flash: the most important thing about becoming bar or bat mitzvah isn't the party. Nor is it the presents. Nor even being able to celebrate with your family and friends—as wonderful as those things are. Nor is it even standing before the congregation and reading the prayers of the liturgy—as important as that is.

No, the most important thing about becoming bar or bat mitzvah is sharing Torah with the congregation. And why is that? Because of all Jewish skills, that is the most important one.

Here is what is true about rites of passage: you can tell what a culture values by the tasks it asks its young people to perform on their way to maturity. In American culture, you become responsible for driving, responsible for voting, and yes, responsible for drinking responsibly.

In some cultures, the rite of passage toward maturity includes some kind of trial, or a test of strength. Sometimes, it is a kind of "outward bound" camping adventure. Among the Maasai tribe in Africa, it is traditional for a young person to hunt and kill a lion. In some Hispanic cultures, fifteen year-old girls celebrate the *quinceañera*, which marks their entrance into maturity.

What is Judaism's way of marking maturity? It combines both of these rites of passage: *responsibility* and *test*. You show that you are on your way to becoming a *responsible* Jewish adult through a public *test* of strength and knowledge—reading or chanting Torah, and then teaching it to the congregation.

This is the most important Jewish ritual mitzvah (commandment), and that is how you demonstrate that you are, truly, bar or bat mitzvah—old enough to be responsible for the mitzvot.

What Is Torah?

So, what exactly is the Torah? You probably know this already, but let's review.

The Torah (teaching) consists of "the five books of Moses," sometimes also called the *chumash* (from the Hebrew word *chameish*, which means "five"), or, sometimes, the Greek word Pentateuch (which means "the five teachings").

Here are the five books of the Torah, with their common names and their Hebrew names.

> **Genesis (The beginning), which in Hebrew is Bere'shit (from the first words—"When God began to create").** Bere'shit spans the years from Creation to Joseph's death in Egypt. Many of the Bible's best stories are in Genesis: the creation story itself; Adam and Eve in the Garden of Eden; Cain and Abel; Noah and the Flood; and the tales of the Patriarchs and Matriarchs, Abraham, Isaac, Jacob, Sarah, Rebekah, Rachel, and Leah. It also includes one of the greatest pieces of world literature, the story of Joseph, which is actually the oldest complete novel in history, comprising more than one-quarter of all Genesis.

> **Exodus (Getting out), which in Hebrew is Shemot (These are the names).** Exodus begins with the story of the Israelite slavery in Egypt. It then moves to the rise of Moses as a leader, and the Israelites' liberation from slavery. After the Israelites leave Egypt, they experience the miracle of the parting of the Sea of Reeds (or "Red Sea"); the giving of the Ten Commandments at Mount Sinai; the idolatry of the Golden Calf; and the design and construction of the Tabernacle and of the ark for the original tablets of the law, which our ancestors carried with them in the desert. Exodus also includes various ethical and civil laws, such as "You shall not wrong a stranger or oppress him, for you were strangers in the land of Egypt" (22:20).

> **Leviticus (about the Levites), or, in Hebrew, Va-yikra' (And God called).** It goes into great detail about the kinds of sacrifices that the ancient Israelites brought as offerings; the laws of ritual purity; the animals that were permitted and forbidden for eating (the beginnings of the tradition of kashrut, the Jewish dietary laws); the diagnosis of various skin diseases; the ethical laws of holiness; the ritual calendar of the Jewish year; and various agricultural laws concerning the treatment of the Land of Israel. Leviticus is basically the manual of ancient Judaism.

> Numbers (because the book begins with the census of the Israelites), or, in Hebrew, Be-midbar (In the wilderness). The book describes the forty years of wandering in the wilderness and the various rebellions against Moses. The constant theme: "Egypt wasn't so bad. Maybe we should go back." The greatest rebellion against Moses was the negative reports of the spies about the Land of Israel, which discouraged the Israelites from wanting to move forward into the land. For that reason, the "wilderness generation" must die off before a new generation can come into maturity and finish the journey.

> Deuteronomy (The repetition of the laws of the Torah), or, in Hebrew, Devarim (The words). The final book of the Torah is, essentially, Moses's farewell address to the Israelites as they prepare to enter the Land of Israel. Here we find various laws that had been previously taught, though sometimes with different wording. Much of Deuteronomy contains laws that will be important to the Israelites as they enter the Land of Israel—laws concerning the establishment of a monarchy and the ethics of warfare. Perhaps the most famous passage from Deuteronomy contains the *Shema,* the declaration of God's unity and uniqueness, and the *Ve-ahavta,* which follows it. Deuteronomy ends with the death of Moses on Mount Nebo as he looks across the Jordan Valley into the land that he will not enter.

Jews read the Torah in sequence—starting with Bere'shit right after Simchat Torah in the autumn, and then finishing Devarim on the following Simchat Torah. Each Torah portion is called a parashah (division; sometimes called a *sidrah,* a place in the order of the Torah reading). The stories go around in a full circle, reminding us that we can always gain more insights and more wisdom from the Torah. This means that if you don't "get" the meaning this year, don't worry—it will come around again.

And What Else? The Haftarah

We read or chant the Torah from the Torah scroll—the most sacred thing that a Jewish community has in its possession. The Torah is written without vowels, and the ability to read it and chant it is part of the challenge and the test.

But there is more to the synagogue reading. Every Torah reading has an accompanying haftarah reading. Haftarah means "conclusion," because there was once a time when the service actually ended with that reading. Some scholars believe that the reading of the haftarah originated at a time when non-Jewish authorities outlawed the reading of the Torah, and the Jews read the haftarah sections instead. In fact, in some synagogues, young people who become bar or bat mitzvah read very little Torah and instead read the entire haftarah portion.

The haftarah portion comes from the Nevi'im, the prophetic books, which are the second part of the Jewish Bible. It is either read or chanted from a Hebrew Bible, or maybe from a booklet or a photocopy.

The ancient sages chose the haftarah passages because their themes reminded them of the words or stories in the Torah text. Sometimes, they chose *haftarah* with special themes in honor of a festival or an upcoming festival.

Not all books in the prophetic section of the Hebrew Bible consist of prophecy. Several are historical. For example:

The book of Joshua tells the story of the conquest and settlement of Israel.

The book of Judges speaks of the period of early tribal rulers who would rise to power, usually for the purpose of uniting the tribes in war against their enemies. Some of these leaders are famous: Deborah, the great prophetess and military leader, and Samson, the biblical strong man.

The books of Samuel start with Samuel, the last judge, and then move to the creation of the Israelite monarchy under Saul and David (approximately 1000 BCE).

The books of Kings tell of the death of King David, the rise of King Solomon, and how the Israelite kingdom split into the Northern Kingdom of Israel and the Southern Kingdom of Judah (approximately 900 BCE).

And then there are the books of the prophets, those spokesmen for God whose words fired the Jewish conscience. Their names are immortal: Isaiah, Jeremiah, Ezekiel, Amos, Hosea, among others.

Someone once said: "There is no evidence of a biblical prophet ever being invited back a second time for dinner." Why? Because the prophets were tough. They had no patience for injustice, apathy, or hypocrisy. No one escaped their criticisms. Here's what they taught:

> God commands the Jews to behave decently toward one another. In fact, God cares more about basic ethics and decency than about ritual behavior.
> God chose the Jews *not* for special privileges, but for special duties to humanity.
> As bad as the Jews sometimes were, there was always the possibility that they would improve their behavior.
> As bad as things might be now, it will not always be that way. Someday, there will be universal justice and peace. Human history is moving forward toward an ultimate conclusion that some call the Messianic Age: a time of universal peace and prosperity for the Jewish people and for all the people of the world.

Your Mission—To Teach Torah to the Congregation

On the day when you become bar or bat mitzvah, you will be reading, or chanting, Torah—in Hebrew. You will be reading, or chanting, the haftarah—in Hebrew. That is the major skill that publicly marks the becoming of bar or bat mitzvah. But, perhaps even more important than that, you need to be able to teach something about the Torah portion, and perhaps the haftarah as well.

And that is where this book comes in. It will be a very valuable resource for you, and your family, in the b'nai mitzvah process.

Here is what you will find in it:

> A brief **summary** of every Torah portion. This is a basic overview of the portion; and, while it might not refer to everything in the Torah portion, it will explain its most important aspects.
> A list of the **major ideas** in the Torah portion. The purpose: to make the Torah portion real, in ways that we can relate to. Every Torah portion contains unique ideas, and when you put all

of those ideas together, you actually come up with a list of Judaism's most important ideas.

> Two *divrei Torah* ("words of Torah," or "sermonettes") for each portion. These *divrei Torah* explain significant aspects of the Torah portion in accessible, reader-friendly language. Each *devar Torah* contains references to **traditional** Jewish sources (those that were written before the modern era), as well as **modern** sources and quotes. We have searched, far and wide, to find sources that are unusual, interesting, and not just the "same old stuff" that many people already know about the Torah portion. Why did we include these minisermons in the volume? Not because we want you to simply copy those sermons and pass them off as your own (that would be cheating), though you are free to quote from them. We included them so that you can see what is possible—how you can try to make meaning for yourself out of the words of Torah.

> **Connections:** This is perhaps the most valuable part. It's a list of questions that you can ask yourself, or that others might help you think about—any of which can lead to the creation of your *devar Torah*.

Note: you don't have to like everything that's in a particular Torah portion. Some aren't that loveable. Some are hard to understand; some are about religious practices that people today might find confusing, and even offensive; some contain ideas that we might find totally outmoded.

But this doesn't have to get in the way. After all, most kids spend a lot of time thinking about stories that contain ideas that modern people would find totally bizarre. Any good medieval fantasy story falls into that category.

And we also believe that, if you spend just a little bit of time with those texts, you can begin to understand what the author was trying to say.

This volume goes one step further. Sometimes, the haftarah comes off as a second thought, and no one really thinks about it. We have tried to solve that problem by including a **summary** of each haftarah, and then a mini-sermon on the haftarah. This will help you learn how these sacred words are relevant to today's world, and even to your own life.

All Bible quotations come from the NJPS translation, which is found in the many different editions of the JPS TANAKH; in the Conservative movement's *Etz Hayim: Torah and Commentary;* in the Reform movement's *Torah: A Modern Commentary;* and in other Bible commentaries and study guides.

How Do I Write a *Devar Torah?*

It really is easier than it looks.

There are many ways of thinking about the *devar Torah.* It is, of course, a short sermon on the meaning of the Torah (and, perhaps, the haftarah) portion. It might even be helpful to think of the *devar Torah* as a "book report" on the portion itself.

The most important thing you can know about this sacred task is: *Learn* the words. *Love* the words. Teach people what it could mean to *live* the words.

Here's a basic outline for a *devar Torah:*

"My Torah portion is (name of portion)_____,
    from the book of _____, chapter

_____.

"In my Torah portion, we learn that_____
    (Summary of portion)
"For me, the most important lesson of this Torah portion is (what
    is the best thing in the portion? Take the portion as a whole;
    your *devar Torah* does not have to be only, or specifically, on the
    verses that you are reading).
"As I learned my Torah portion, I found myself wondering:
    › *Raise a question that the Torah portion itself raises.*
    › *"Pick a fight"* with the portion. Argue with it.
    › *Answer a question* that is listed in the "Connections" section of
      each Torah portion.
    › *Suggest a question to your rabbi* that you would want the rabbi
      to answer in his or her own *devar Torah* or sermon.

"I have lived the values of the Torah by _____
(here, you can talk about how the Torah portion relates to your
own life. If you have done a mitzvah project, you can talk about
that here).

How To Keep It from Being Boring
(and You from Being Bored)

Some people just don't like giving traditional speeches. From our per-
spective, that's really okay. Perhaps you can teach Torah in a different
way—one that makes sense to you.

> ➤ Write an "open letter" to one of the characters in your Torah por-
> tion. "Dear Abraham: I hope that your trip to Canaan was not too
> hard . . ." "Dear Moses: Were you afraid when you got the Ten
> Commandments on Mount Sinai? I sure would have been . . ."
> ➤ Write a news story about what happens. Imagine yourself to
> be a television or news reporter. "Residents of neighboring cit-
> ies were horrified yesterday as the wicked cities of Sodom and
> Gomorrah were burned to the ground. Some say that God was
> responsible . . ."
> ➤ Write an imaginary interview with a character in your Torah portion.
> ➤ Tell the story from the point of view of another character, or a mi-
> nor character, in the story. For instance, tell the story of the Gar-
> den of Eden from the point of view of the serpent. Or the story
> of the Binding of Isaac from the point of view of the ram, which
> was substituted for Isaac as a sacrifice. Or perhaps the story of
> the sale of Joseph from the point of view of his coat, which was
> stripped off him and dipped in a goat's blood.
> ➤ Write a poem about your Torah portion.
> ➤ Write a song about your Torah portion.
> ➤ Write a play about your Torah portion, and have some friends act
> it out with you.
> ➤ Create a piece of artwork about your Torah portion.

The bottom line is: Make this a joyful experience. Yes—it could
even be fun.

The Very Last Thing You Need to Know at This Point

The Torah scroll is written without vowels. Why? Don't *sofrim* (Torah scribes) know the vowels?

Of course they do.

So, why do they leave the vowels out?

One reason is that the Torah came into existence at a time when sages were still arguing about the proper vowels, and the proper pronunciation.

But here is another reason: The Torah text, as we have it today, and as it sits in the scroll, is actually *an unfinished work*. Think of it: the words are just sitting there. Because they have no vowels, it is as if they have no voice.

When we read the Torah publicly, we give voice to the ancient words. And when we find meaning in those ancient words, and we talk about those meanings, those words jump to life. They enter our lives. They make our world deeper and better.

Mazal tov to you, and your family. This is your journey toward Jewish maturity. Love it.

THE TORAH

❖ Mikkets: Genesis 41:1–44:17

The Joseph drama, part 2. Joseph, the dreamer, morphs into Joseph, the dream interpreter. Pharaoh has a series of troubling dreams, and Joseph is summoned from the dungeon to interpret them. This turns out to be an ideal career move. Joseph becomes second in power only to Pharaoh, and helps Egypt prepare for the coming famine.

His brothers come down to Egypt to buy grain and run into Joseph, but they don't recognize him. Joseph wonders if the brothers have changed, if he can really trust them now, and so he puts them through various (somewhat cruel) trials to test them. Will he reveal his identity? Then what will happen?

Summary

- › Joseph interprets the dreams of Pharaoh, and Pharaoh rewards him by releasing him from jail and inviting him to take charge of the Egyptian economy and to protect the country from famine. (41:1–44)
- › Joseph acquires an Egyptian name and marries into an influential Egyptian family. He and his wife, Asenath, have two sons—Ephraim and Manasseh. (41:45–46,50-52)
- › When the famine hits Canaan, Joseph's brothers come down to Egypt to purchase grain. They don't realize that the powerful man they are dealing with is actually their long-lost brother, Joseph. Joseph imprisons them on trumped-up spying charges. Ultimately, he lets them go—on the condition that they bring his youngest brother, Benjamin, to him. (42:1–17)
- › The famine continues, and the brothers return to Egypt with Benjamin. (43:1–34)
- › As the brothers prepare to return to Canaan, Joseph puts his silver goblet in Benjamin's bag, and accuses the brothers of being thieves. (44:1–17)

The Big Ideas

> **Assimilation is always a temptation for Jews.** Joseph assimilates in Egypt. In some ways, he becomes like a regular Egyptian. In others, he is still Jewish. He has a foot in two cultures, like modern Jews who are both deeply American (or Canadian, or British) and deeply Jewish.

> **Actions always have consequences.** Joseph reorganizes the Egyptian economy. But, in doing so, he turns the Egyptian people into slaves to Pharaoh. Years later, this will happen to the Israelites in Egypt as well. As we have already seen: what goes around, comes around.

> **Life is filled with tests of character.** That was what Joseph was doing to his brothers—seeing if they had really changed (and there may be some pure vengeance going on as well!). Joseph tightens the screws by framing Benjamin. The stakes for all involved have just been raised.

> **Showing emotion is healthy for everybody.** Joseph shows more emotion than almost anyone else in the Bible. He cries—out of sadness, longing, and even joy. Mature men and women can show their emotions, and it is often good to do so.

Divrei Torah

JOSEPH'S SECRET IDENTITY

Many people do not know that a handful of Jewish men invented the comic-book industry. In fact, the most famous comic-book characters were created by Jews: Superman (by Joe Shuster and Jerry Siegel) and Batman (by Bob Kane).

Perhaps the strangest thing about super heroes is that they have secret identities. Superman is really Clark Kent. Batman is really Bruce Wayne. Ever wonder if they get confused—"who am I really, at this moment?" And, really—how dumb were the people of Metropolis and Gotham City? They couldn't figure out who Superman and Batman really were? Do you think that Batman's mask made a difference? And Superman—who couldn't figure out that Superman and Clark Kent were one and the same person?

That's the way it is with Joseph. When he gets out of prison, he not only sheds his prison garb. He gets a new set of clothing and, with it, a new identity. Pharaoh changes his name to Zaphenath-paneah. To quote a medieval commentator: "If that name is Egyptian, then we don't know what it means! In any case, Pharaoh wanted to honor Joseph by giving him an Egyptian name. If it is Hebrew, then it could mean 'the revealer of secret things.'" Joseph marries Asenath, the daughter of Poti-phera, the high priest of the sun god (not to be confused with Potiphar, who had earlier bought Joseph as a slave).

Did Joseph ever wonder who he really was? Hebrew—or Egyptian?

Sometimes it seems that Joseph is really Egyptian. He looks so Egyptian that his brothers don't recognize him. He marries an Egyptian woman, whose father was a very powerful priest of one of Egypt's main gods. He moves through the corridors of power in Egyptian society. And, during all his years in Egypt, he never "phones home," even to tell his poor father, Jacob, that he is still alive.

And, sometimes it seems that Joseph is really a Hebrew. Yes, he was married to the daughter of a major Egyptian priest, but some ancient writers thought that Asenath converted to Judaism. Yes, Joseph's father-in-law, Poti-phera, was heavily involved with worshiping the sun, but Joseph is never portrayed as following his example. Finally, Joseph reunites with his Hebrew family, travels back to Canaan to bury his father, and names his sons Ephraim and Manasseh—Hebrew names.

Joseph lived in two cultures—Hebrew and Egyptian. He is the forerunner of the modern American Jew, who lives in two cultures at the same time—American and Jewish. To quote Mordecai Kaplan: "Jews live in two civilizations, in their own and in the countries in which they live, and they want those two civilizations to play an equal part in their lives."

So, who is Joseph? In many respects, isn't he like us?

WHY DOES JOSEPH MESS WITH HIS BROTHERS?

We can only imagine Joseph's brothers saying the following under their breaths: "All right, we know that this guy is very important here in Egypt. We got that. But, why is he being such a jerk to us?"

Ever since Joseph recognized his brothers, who had come down to Egypt to buy grain during the famine in the Land of Israel, he has been really messing with their heads. He accuses them of being spies. He demands that they bring their youngest brother, Benjamin, down to Egypt. He ties his brother Simeon up in front of them. When they come back to Egypt to buy food again, he puts his silver cup into Benjamin's bag and accuses them of being thieves. He then demands that Benjamin should remain with him as his slave.

Why is Joseph doing this to his brothers? Was it simply payback for what they had done to him, years before? Or, perhaps he was testing them. He wanted to see if they would stick up for their younger brother, Benjamin. Would they treat him better than they had treated him?

Even though Joseph is clearly in charge here, and even though he is actually bullying his brothers, they don't cry. No—the only one who cries is Joseph—a lot. Is it because he was so moved to see them again, and how they had aged? Was he remembering how he had suffered at their hands? Was he thinking about all the years that they had missed together? Was he pained to see how much anger he still had inside him?

Rabbi Morris Adler suggests that Joseph cries because he realizes how much power he now has, and how easy it is to abuse that power and to become overly arrogant about it. "Privilege is in danger of giving us a sense of personal quality and egotism that puts us far above the common man and feeds our vanity with the most destructive illusions."

Perhaps Joseph is moved to tears because he saw that his brothers had truly repented. They could have given up Benjamin to him, but they didn't. In the words of the great medieval philosopher Maimonides: "What constitutes complete repentance? If someone finds himself in the same situation in which he had previously sinned, and if he could commit the sin again, but he doesn't do it again, then we know that this person has truly repented."

But there is yet another possibility. Perhaps Joseph is moved by how much his brothers demonstrate that they care for each other and for their aged father. It had not always been that way. Joseph had been the victim of their lack of caring, and so had their father.

But his brothers had changed, and that was reason enough for Joseph to cry. This time, in joy.

Connections

> Have you ever had odd or interesting dreams? Have you thought about what they might mean?

> What things that you love to do are Jewish? Which are American? Do you ever feel you need to choose one over the other?

> Has your character ever been tested? When was it tough to decide right from wrong?

> Do you agree that Joseph was bullying his brothers? Could he have handled things differently?

> Have you ever been in a situation where you did something wrong, and then chose not to do so again? Or perhaps you did do it again and regretted it?

> When is it okay for grownups to cry publicly?

THE HAFTARAH

❖ Mikkets: 1 Kings 3:15–28; 4:1

What is up with the way that people in the Bible treat children? First, Abraham almost sacrifices his son Isaac. And, now, Solomon almost kills an infant!

Well, not exactly. This haftarah opens with a king awakening from a dream—just like the Torah portion, in which Pharaoh had a disturbing dream and needed to find out its meaning. Here, King Solomon has just become king of Israel, after the death of his father, David, and he dreams that he is being blessed with wisdom. Now he has to prove it.

Two women—prostitutes, actually—bring two infants to the king—one alive and the other dead. Each woman claims that the live child is hers. Solomon orders that a sword be brought to him, so that he can cut the live child in half and give half to each woman. At this, the real mother shouts out: "Please, my lord . . . give her the live child; only don't kill it!" (3:26). That was how Solomon knew who the real mother was—because she would rather see the child live, even with another mother, than die.

This is one of the most famous stories in the Bible. It is the source of the phrase "a Solomonic decision." It may have been a wise decision, but what would have happened if the real mother hadn't spoke up? Wisdom is always put to the test.

Can Solomon "Cut It" as King?

What does it mean to be smart? You probably think that it has something to do with getting good grades—"She's the smartest girl in the class." Okay. But what does it mean to be wise? That's something different. There are probably many smart people who aren't necessarily wise, and some wise people who aren't smart. You can measure smart, perhaps, with an IQ test. Wise is something else.

Solomon was wise. In fact, he is considered the wisest person in the Bible. The Bible itself doesn't give many examples of this wisdom except for his first act as king; Solomon doesn't fight a battle or make a decision about taxes. He acts as a judge, and he really has to use his legendary wisdom.

The two women enter. They have no names; they don't even know each other's names. There is a live child and a dead child. Rabbi Zoe Klein imagines how the woman with the dead child must have felt: "The boy is dead. She believes that she suffocated him in the night by rolling over in her sleep. And so the woman is struck all at once by an enormity of grief and guilt."

How did Solomon know which mother was the real mother? A midrash teaches that a *bat kol* (a heavenly voice) came forth from heaven, identifying the real mother. But, as other sages note, maybe it was his intuition or his careful observation or his listening skills that led him to the truth.

Rabbi Joseph Kara, a medieval commentator, observes that the first woman said that three days separated the boys' births. Perhaps Solomon noticed that the older baby looked just a bit more physically developed.

Another medieval commentator, Isaac Abravanel, suggests that Solomon studied the facial expression, manner of speaking, and body language of each woman, and that was how he knew the answer. In other words, he heard not only the facts of the case; he had the skill to look beyond the facts and to really see into the hearts of the women.

The modern commentator Malbim notices that one woman mentioned the live child first and the dead child second. The real mother would have done that because the live child would have been foremost on her mind. That is why Solomon is said to have a "listening heart."

Wisdom is not only having a high IQ. It's having a heart and not just a brain. It's about knowing the facts but likewise having the ability to judge with fairness. The story concludes, "Solomon was now king over all Israel" (4:1). To win over everyone, a great king must be a wise king.

❖ Notes

❖ Notes